How People Got Wisdom

An Ashanti Tale

retold by Benjamin Khan
illustrated by Marla Baggetta

 HOUGHTON MIFFLIN   BOSTON

Long, long ago, no one in the world had any wisdom. Creatures just wandered around, trying to understand what life was all about. Sometimes they would learn new skills, but they quickly forgot them. Everyone just struggled through life.

Anansi the spider wasn't wise, but neither was anyone else.

One day, Nyame visited Anansi's web. Nyame was the god of the sky. The spider rarely had guests, so this was an unexpected pleasure.

"Hello, my friend," said Nyame. "I thought you might like some company. I have brought you some sweet yams and a golden thread for your web." The sky god also carried a pot under his arm.

Anansi reached for the treats, but the sky god continued speaking. "I would like a small favor in return, if you please."

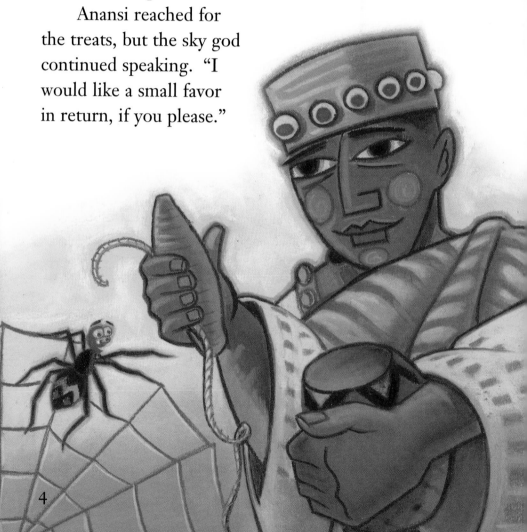

Nyame pointed to the pot he carried and said,
"Wisdom is in this pot, all the wisdom in the world.
Would you please take it and share it with everyone else?
I would do it myself, but I feel a thunderstorm coming,
and I need to get ready."

Now, Anansi was lazy and didn't really want to help. Still, he was flattered to be asked. He was also very curious about the contents of the pot, so he agreed to the request.

As soon as his visitor left, Anansi pried off the pot lid and peered inside. "Oh, my!" he said, whistling.

The pot contained many wonderful secrets. Anansi sifted through them carefully, gaining wisdom by the minute.

He learned where fat flies sleep and how to catch them. He learned how to weave bright threads into cloth. He learned how to make colorful pottery. He learned where gold could be mined from the ground. He even learned how to gather plantains and how to make yams grow larger and sweeter.

At first, Anansi had planned to share this wisdom with others, as Nyame had requested. However, when he saw all the secrets, he became greedy.

Why should I give any of this wisdom away? he thought. *I should keep all this knowledge for myself!*

Then Anansi started to worry. What if another animal saw his pot, lifted the lid, and looked inside? He didn't want that to happen, so he decided to hide the pot.

Should he hide it in the river? No, surely the river would overflow its banks, and the pot would be lost.

Should he hide it on the plains? No, a grass fire would certainly sweep across the plains, and the pot would be destroyed.

He scratched his head and thought some more.

Just then, Anansi noticed a tall tree growing in the jungle nearby. "Aha!" he thought. "I will hide this pot up in this tree, where no one else will see it."

Grasping the heavy pot firmly, he started climbing. Anansi didn't get very high, for the smooth pot kept sliding out of his grasp.

"This is not going to work," he said. "I need all eight hands just to hang on to this slippery thing."

He returned to the ground and thought for a minute. Then he poured the wisdom into a gourd, which he fastened to his waist with rope. "That ought to do it!" he said, smiling.

Once again, he started climbing. First the swinging gourd jabbed him in the stomach. Then it bumped his chin. Later, it poked him in his favorite eye.

12

Anansi looked up the tree and saw how far he still had to go. Then he looked down at his bruises.

"This isn't going to work, either," he muttered. By now, he was getting cross. He was also starting to feel a little sorry for himself.

Just then, a young girl passed by the tree. She looked up and waved. Anansi scowled at her.

"Why are you angry?" she asked.

Anansi hesitated and then said, "I'm trying to reach the top of this tree, but this gourd keeps getting in my way. Just look at these bruises!"

"I have an idea," the girl said. "Tie the gourd tightly onto your back. Then, it won't be in your way, and you can climb up easily."

Anansi stared at her as if *she* had eight arms. Why hadn't he thought of that?

I have all the wisdom, Anansi thought, *yet I couldn't solve my problem. This child solved it easily.*

Anansi wondered why he was having such a hard time. Was it because he hadn't followed Nyame's directions about what to do with the pot?

Anansi frowned. *Why am I going to all this trouble?* he asked himself. He looked up at the sky and shook several fists. "Here's what I think of your wisdom!" he shouted to the sky god. Furious, he threw the gourd down.

The gourd hit the ground and shattered. Bits of wisdom flew everywhere. The wind picked up pieces and carried them all over the world. Then people found them and took them home.

Today, you can find wisdom everywhere. Everyone in the world has at least a little bit of it. Wise people, who have a greater share of wisdom than others, have learned to share what they know. As a result, no one has it all.

In this way, the wish of Nyame, the sky god, was finally carried out. Everyone in the world shares all the wisdom in the world.